For Jason and Emma

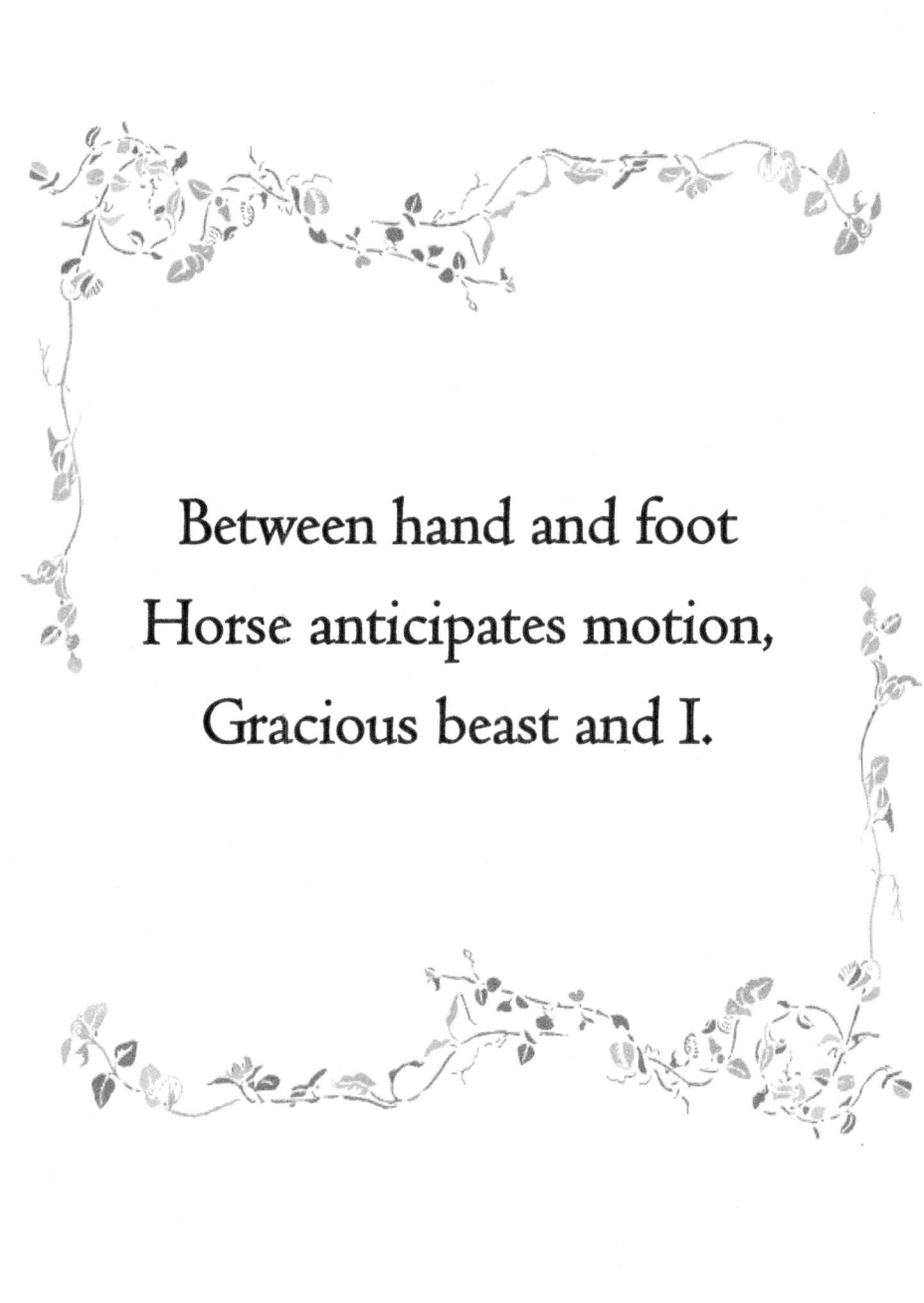

Between hand and foot
Horse anticipates motion,
Gracious beast and I.

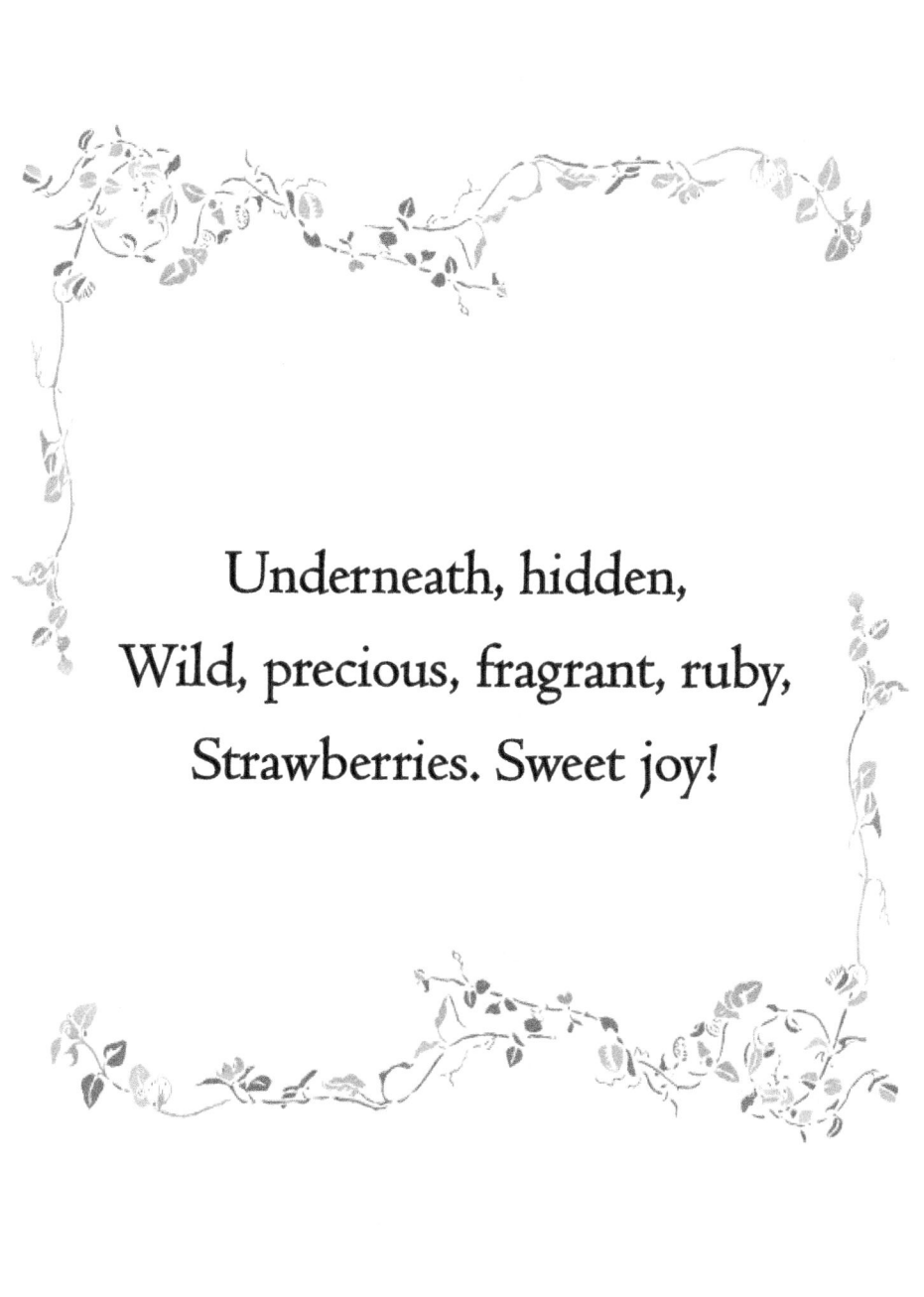

Underneath, hidden,
Wild, precious, fragrant, ruby,
Strawberries. Sweet joy!

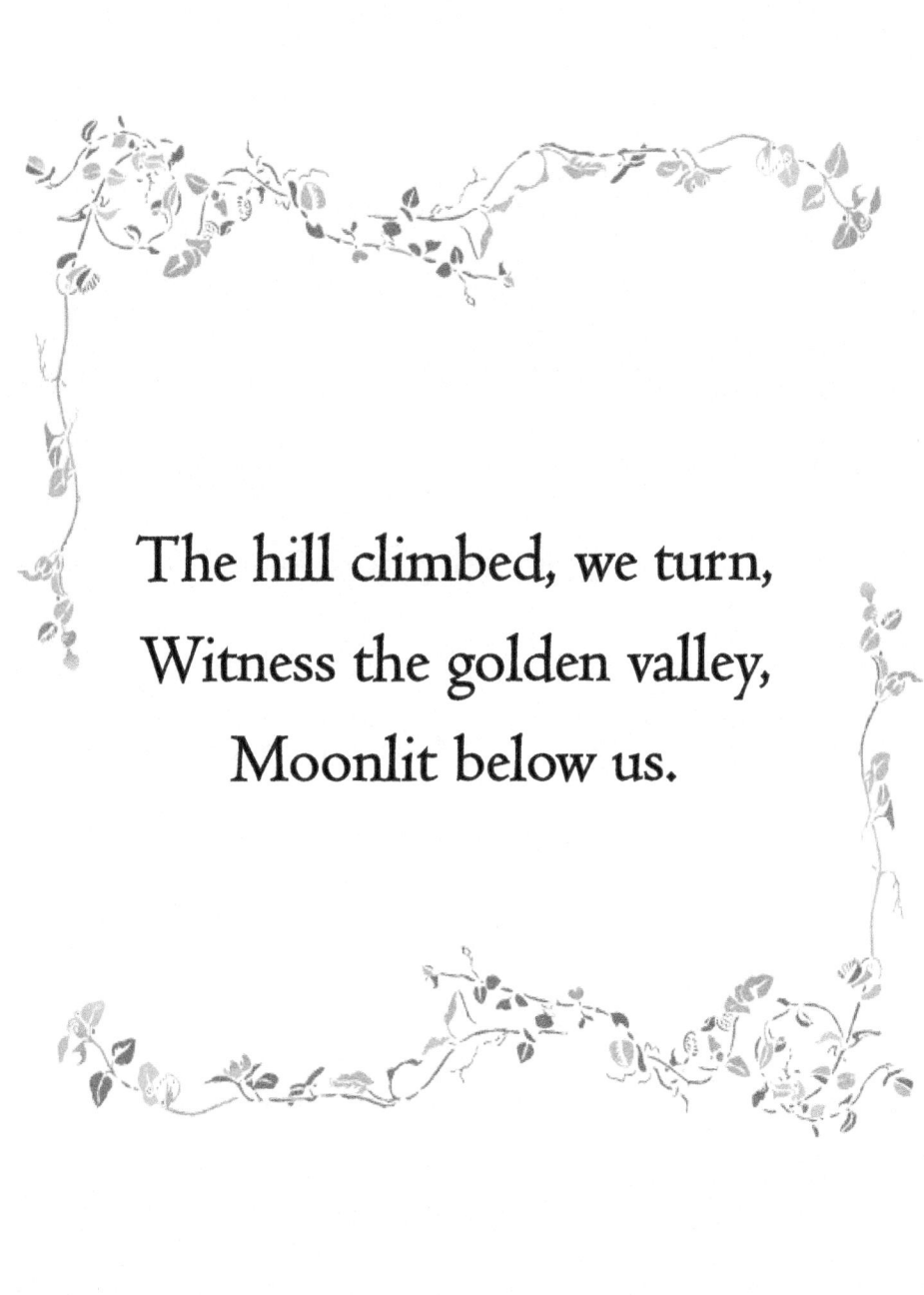

The hill climbed, we turn,
Witness the golden valley,
Moonlit below us.

My bedroom window,
Frames starry night sky beyond,
The world keeps turning.

Sun leaves the sky, dips,

Below distant horizon,

Red embrace lingers.

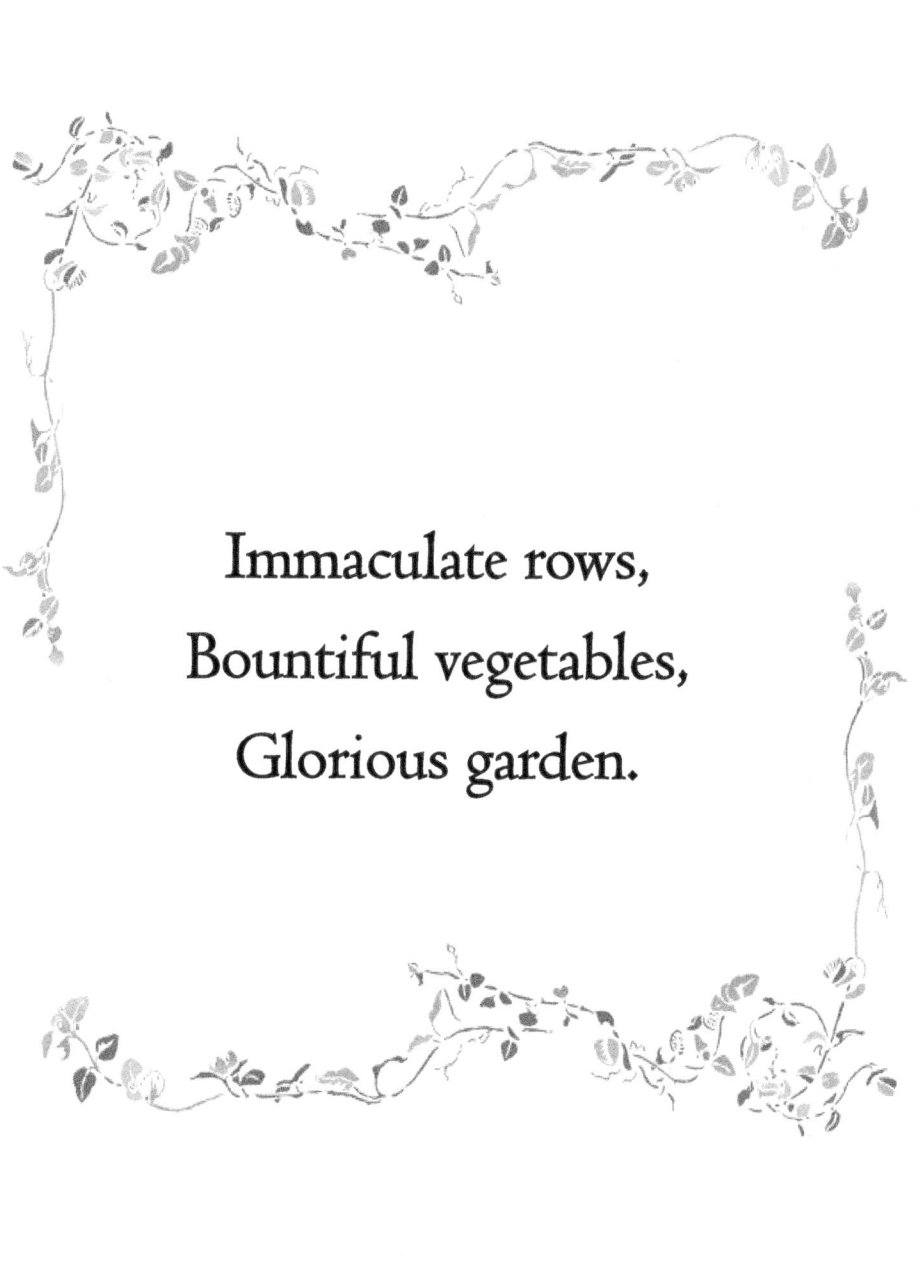

Immaculate rows,

Bountiful vegetables,

Glorious garden.

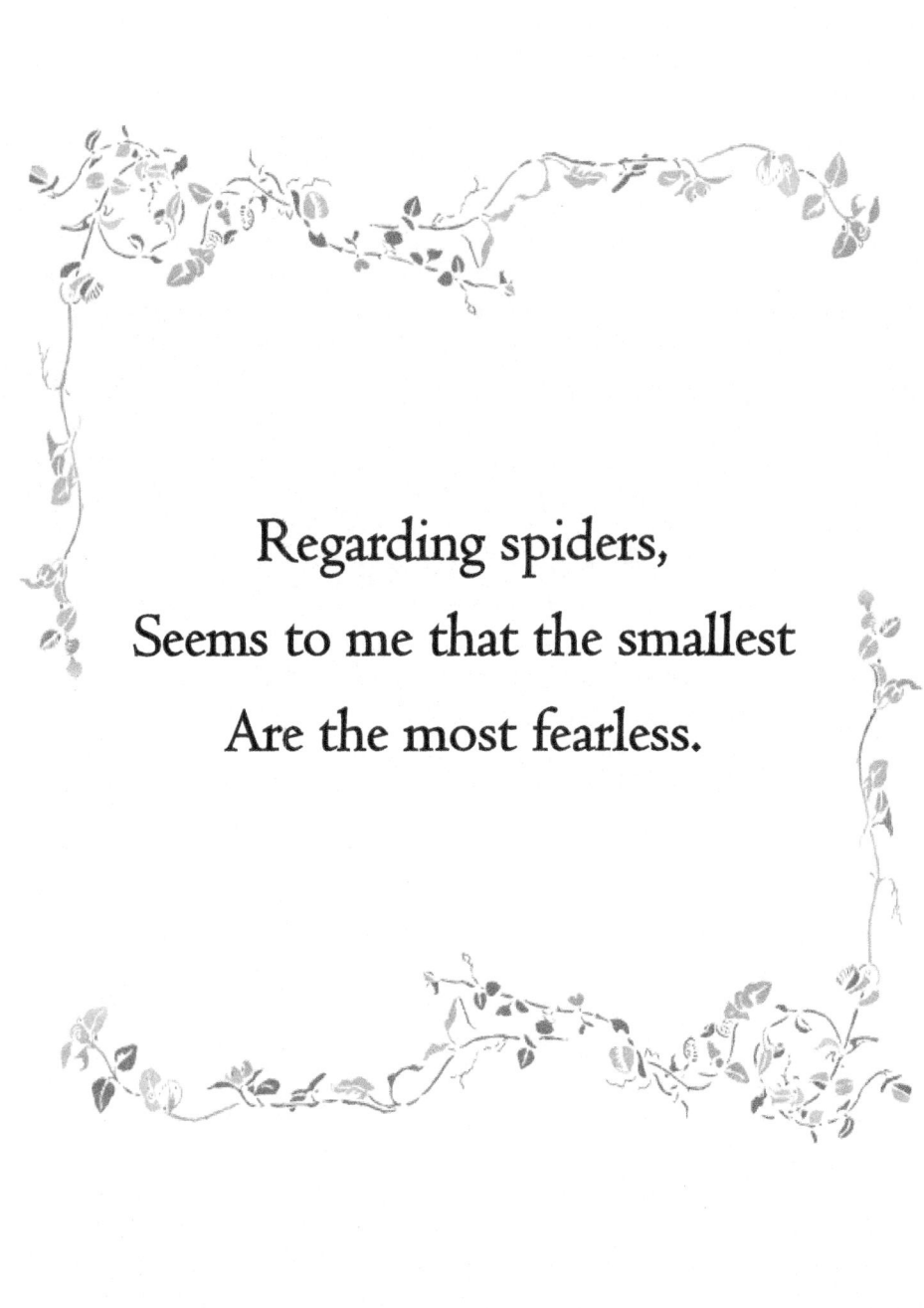

Regarding spiders,

Seems to me that the smallest

Are the most fearless.

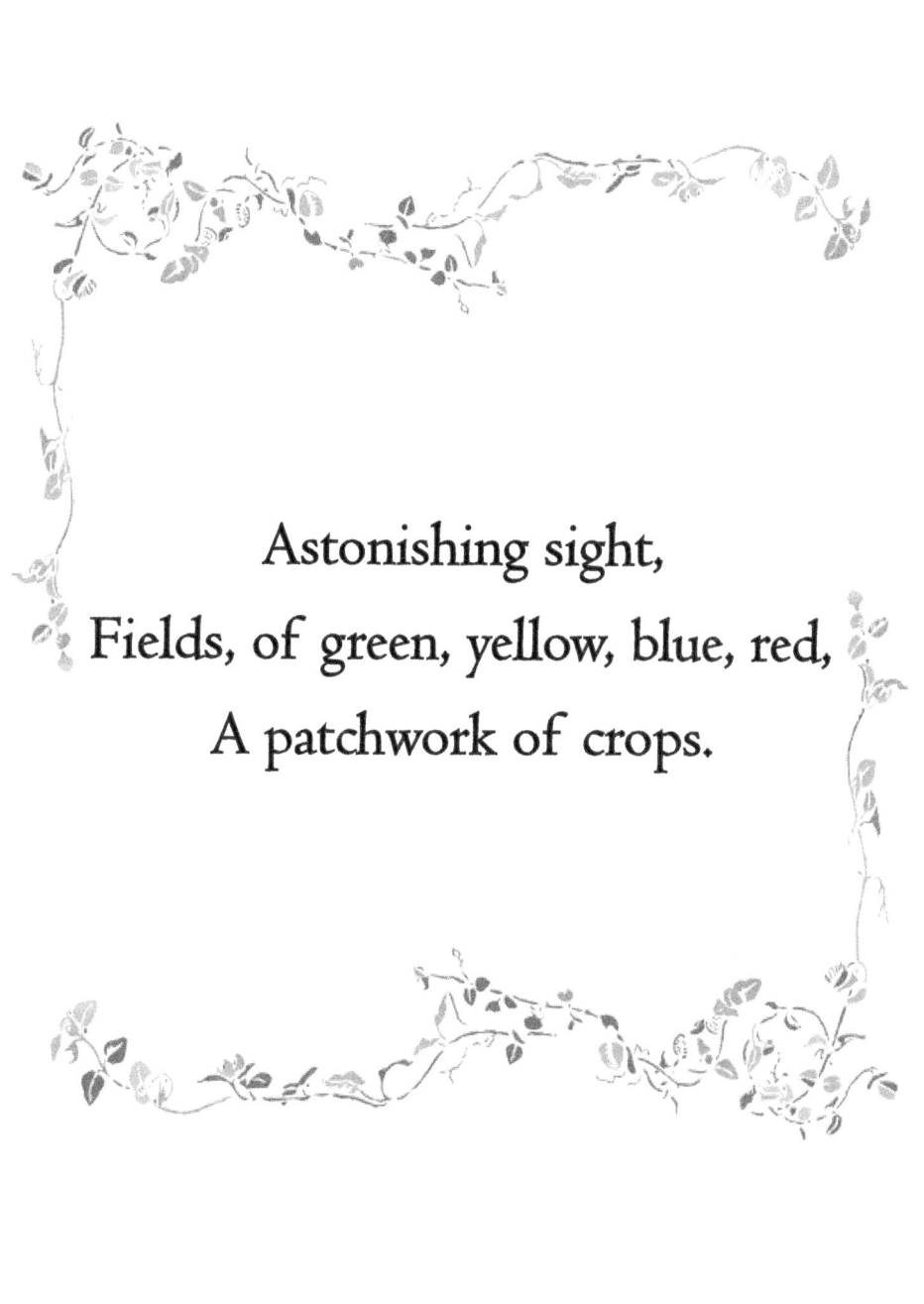

Astonishing sight,
Fields, of green, yellow, blue, red,
A patchwork of crops.

Golden bird races,

We hurtle down country lanes,

Fleeting companion.

Canopy of leaves,
I exist in dappled light.
Luminosity.

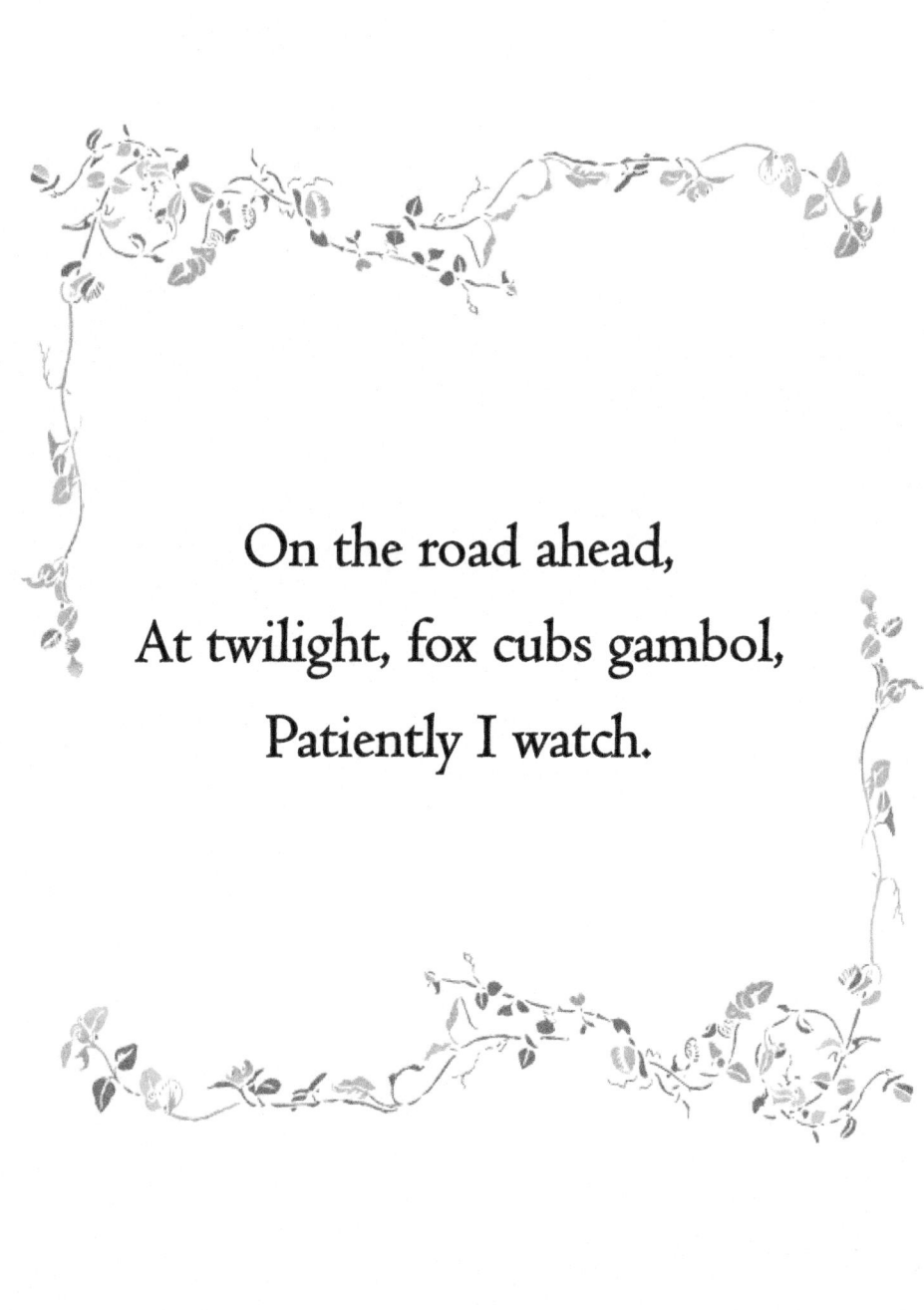

On the road ahead,

At twilight, fox cubs gambol,

Patiently I watch.

The snow plough's been through,
Liberated the village,
And left snow mountains.

Magical lanterns,

Suspended on the long grass,

The glow worms glimmer.

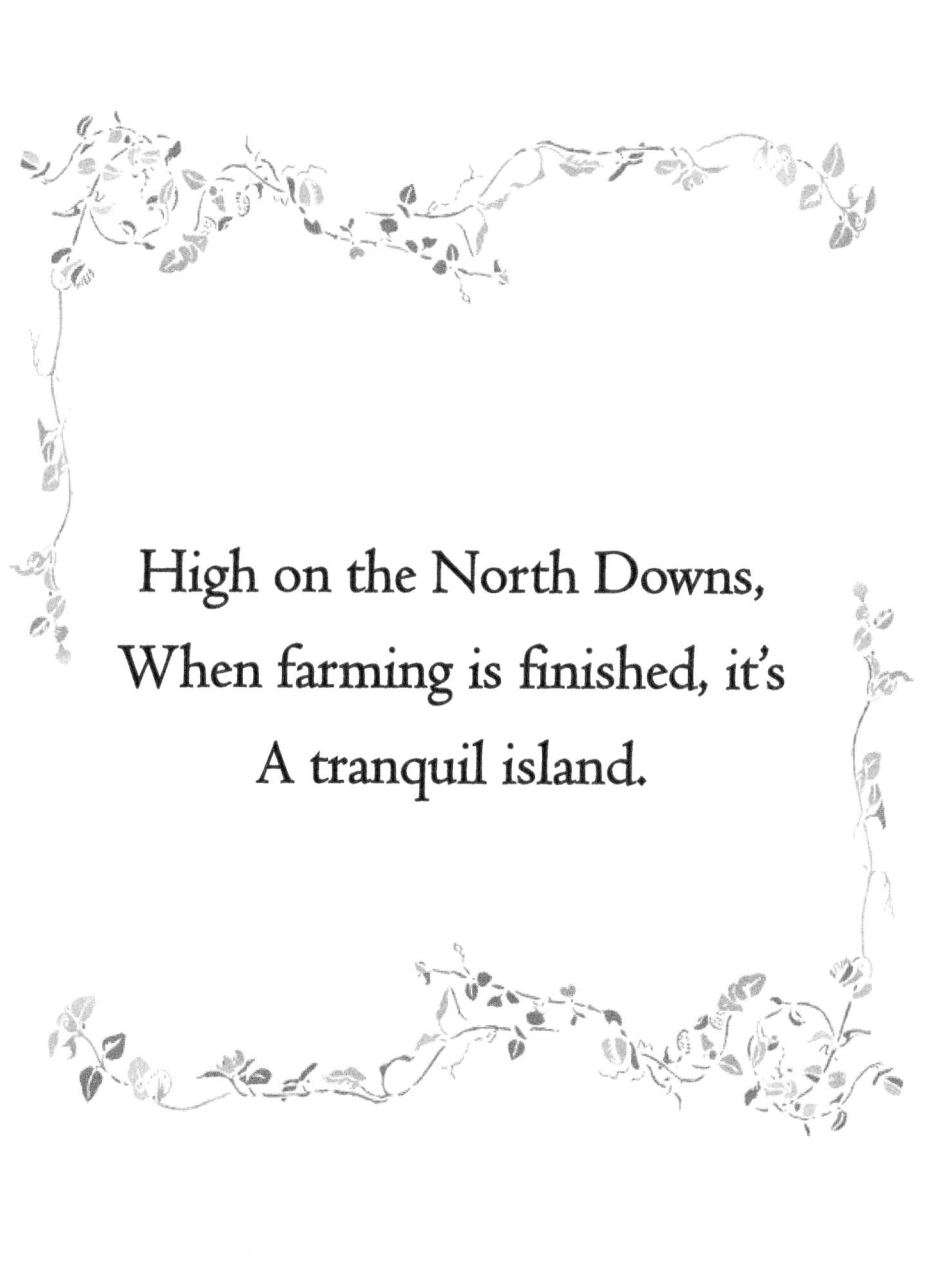

High on the North Downs,
When farming is finished, it's
A tranquil island.

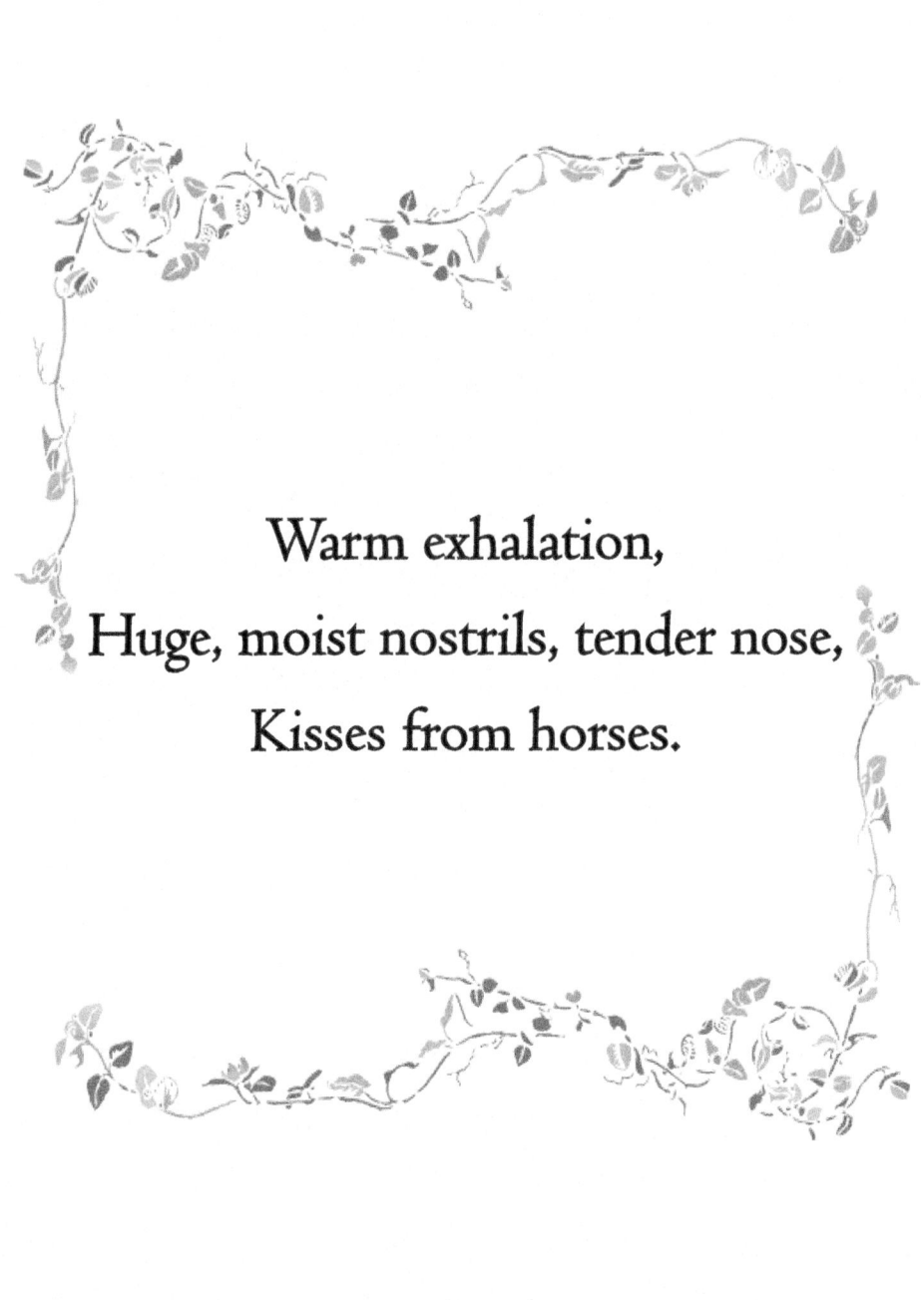

Warm exhalation,

Huge, moist nostrils, tender nose,

Kisses from horses.

The cat's been hunting,
Bloodbath in the dining room,
What joy to clean up.

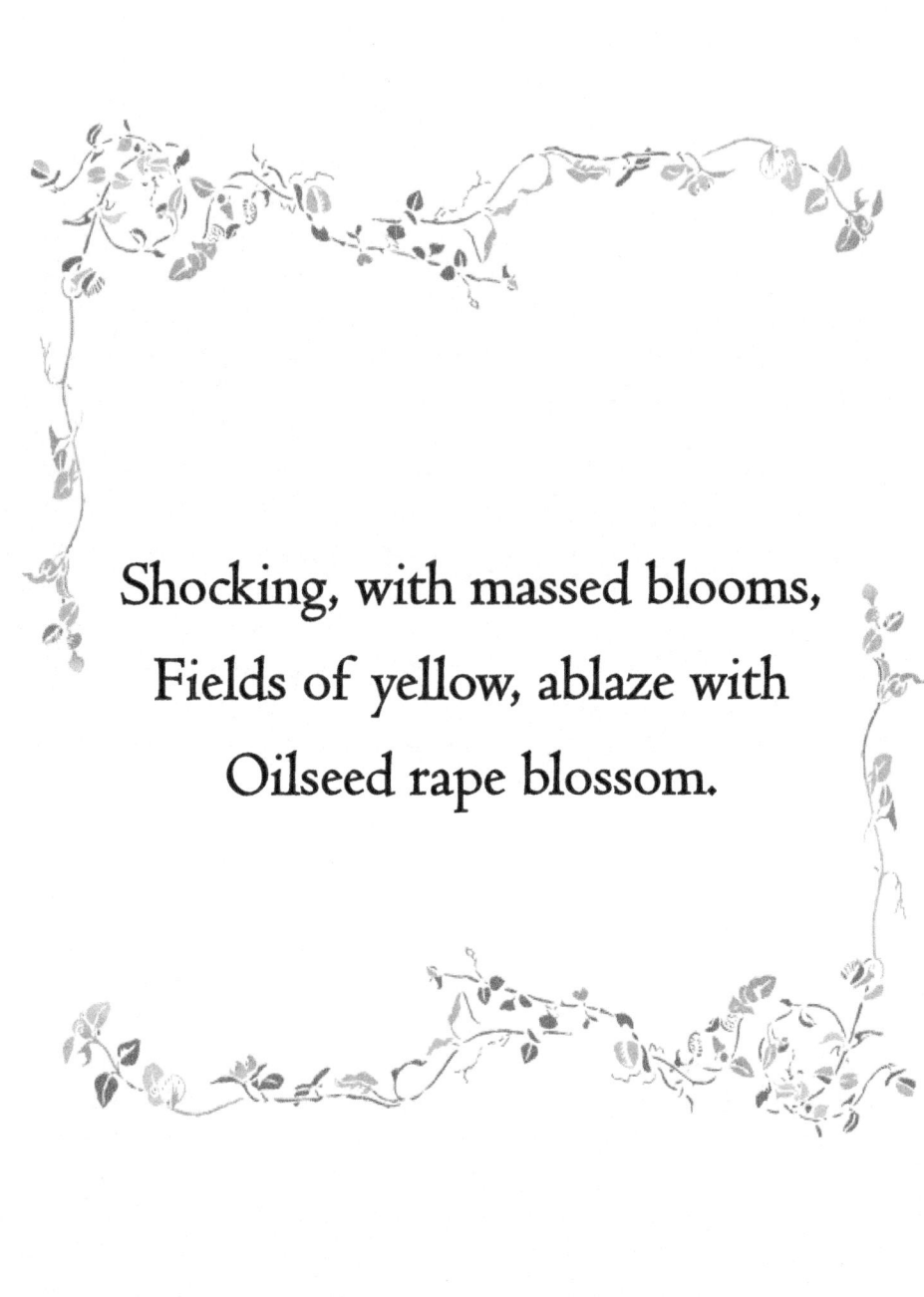

Shocking, with massed blooms,

Fields of yellow, ablaze with

Oilseed rape blossom.

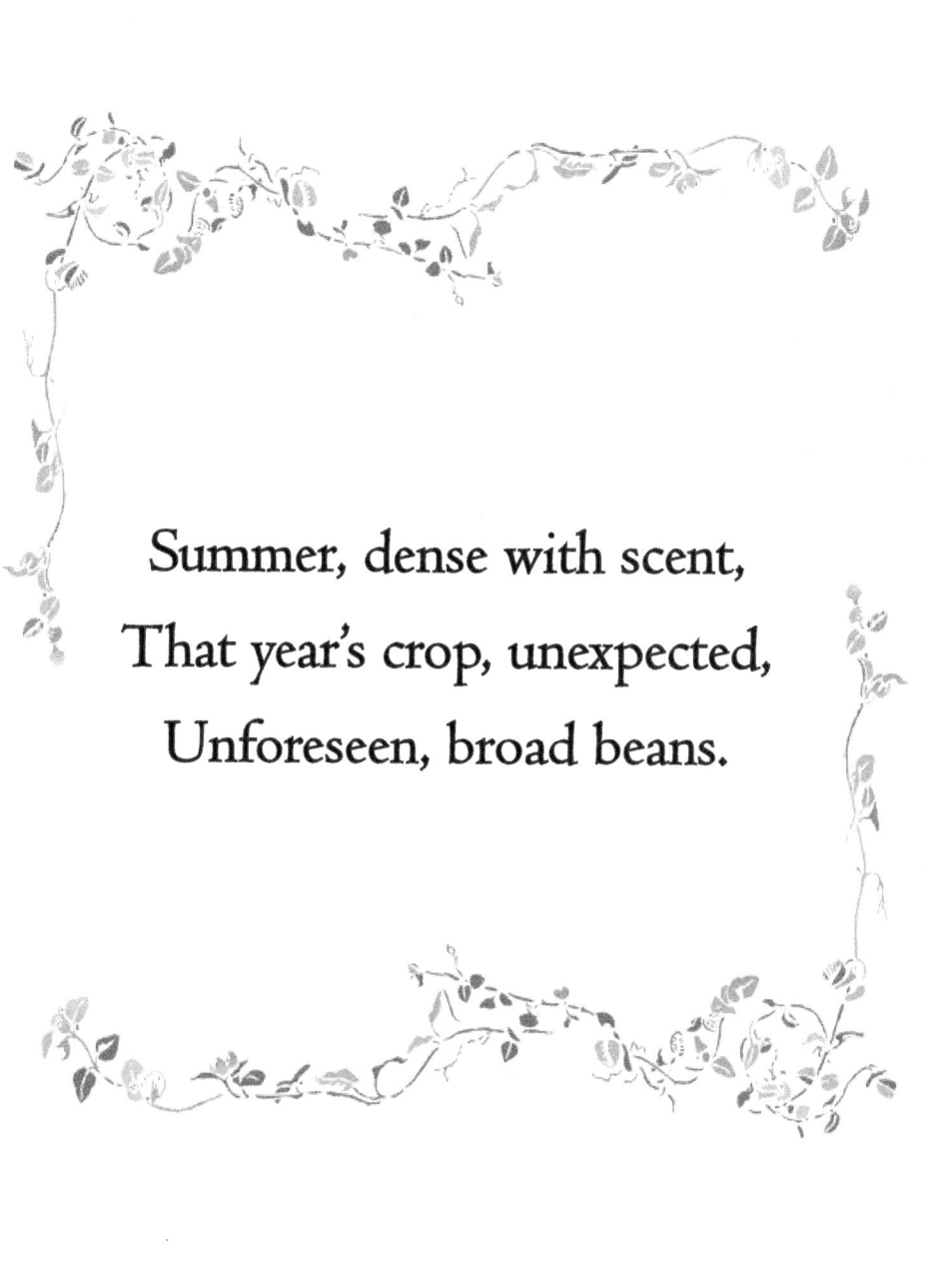

Summer, dense with scent,

That year's crop, unexpected,

Unforeseen, broad beans.

Clear, cold, crisp night sky,
Stars gleam fiercely, lights wink from
Aircraft overhead.

Beautiful brown earth,
Freshly ploughed, in neat furrows,
Promise of harvest.

It's a party when
The power's out- the pub has
A generator!

There's a farm, next door,
To the village school, in spring
Lambs and kids abound.

Tiny, feathery,

Quails, mother and chicks, in line,

Scutter down the road.

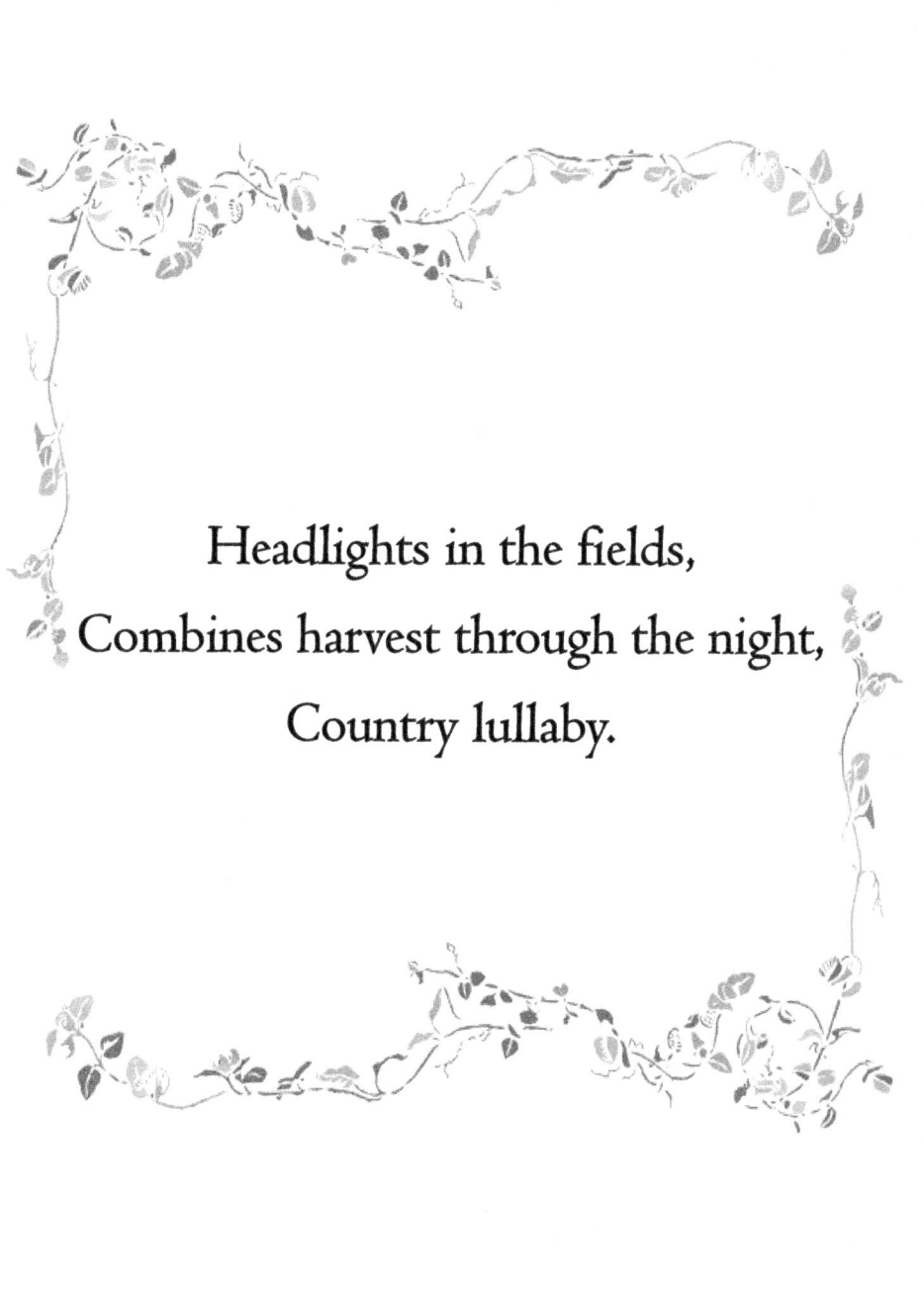

Headlights in the fields,
Combines harvest through the night,
Country lullaby.

Still, summer evening,
A dog barks, far away, there
Is no other sound.

A mystical spell,

Stag and I, frozen. Could have

Reached out and touched him.

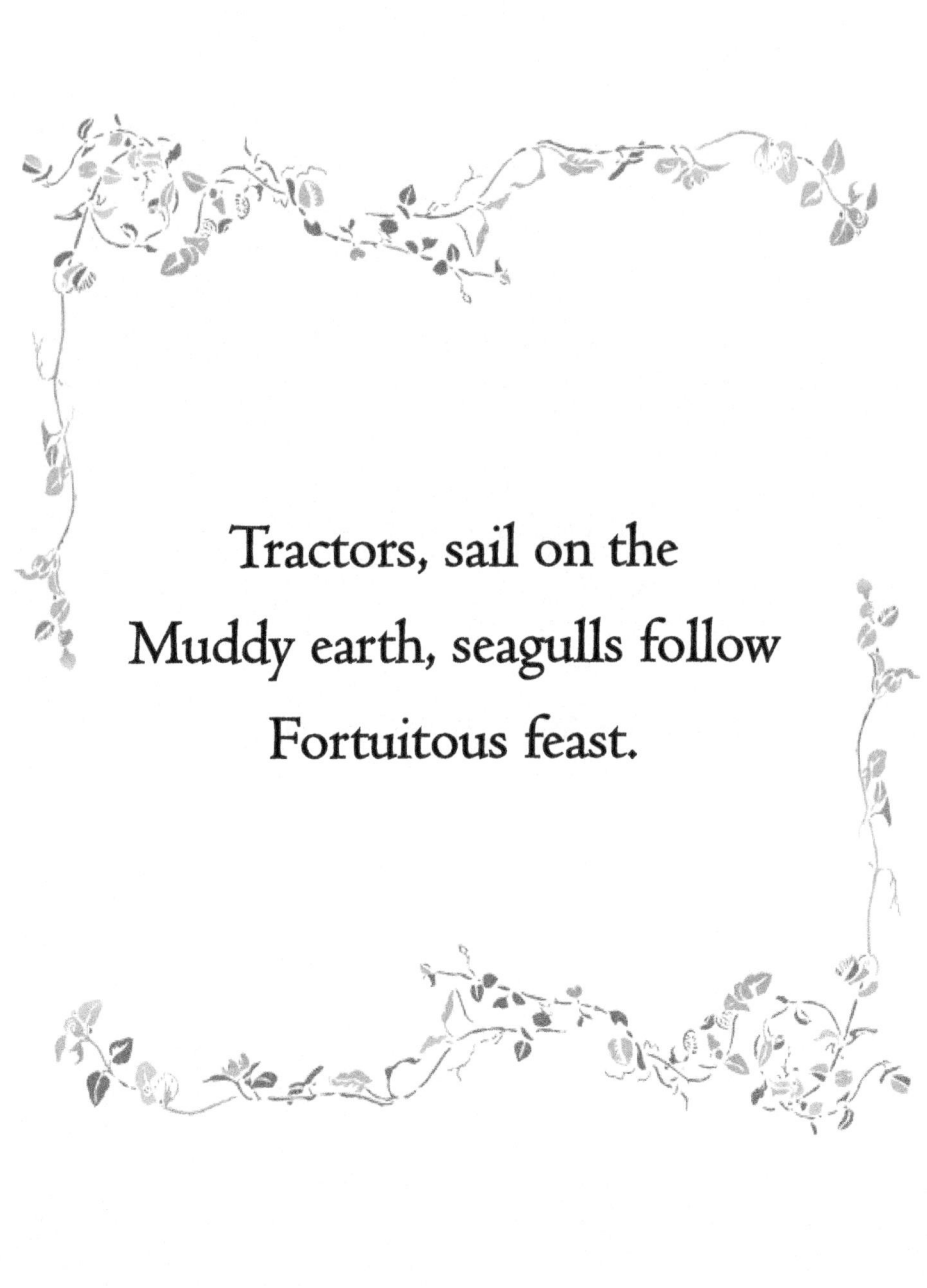

Tractors, sail on the
Muddy earth, seagulls follow
Fortuitous feast.

Two ponies, four dogs,
Four kids, two bikes, mums deserve
A pub garden drink.

Circumstances, that
Led to goats in the churchyard,
Can't be explained here!

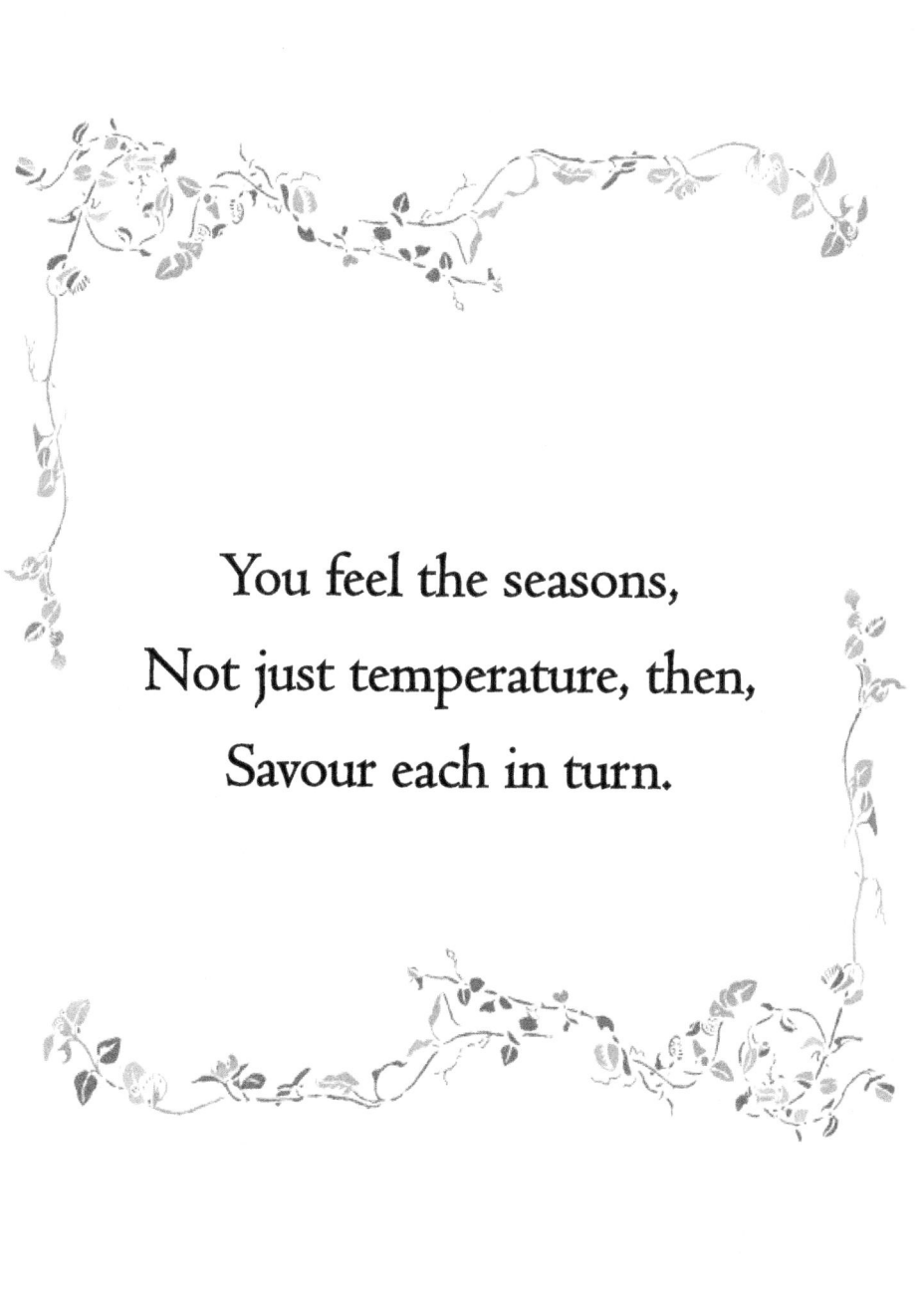

You feel the seasons,

Not just temperature, then,

Savour each in turn.

Printed in Great Britain
by Amazon